CHARLIE BROWN

VIOLET

SHERMY

PATTY

LINUS

SNOOPY

SCHROEDER

'PIG-PEN'

LUCY

THE WONDERFUL

WORLD OF PEANUTS

Selected Cartoons From
more **PEANUTS**.
VOL 1

by Charles M. Schulz

A FAWCETT CREST BOOK

Fawcett Publications, Inc., Greenwich, Conn.

Member of American Book Publishers Council, Inc.

Other PEANUTS Books in Fawcett Crest Editions:

Only 50¢ Each—Wherever Paperbacks Are Sold

If your dealer is sold out, send only cover price plus 10¢ each for postage and handling to Crest Books, Fawcett Publications, Inc., Greenwich, Conn. 06830. Please order by number and title. If five or more books are ordered, there is no postage or handling charge. No Canadian orders. Catalog available on request.

THE WONDERFUL WORLD OF PEANUTS

This book, prepared especially for Fawcett Publications, Inc., comprises the first half of MORE PEANUTS, and is reprinted by arrangement with Holt, Rinehart and Winston, Inc.

Seventeenth Fawcett Crest printing, October 1969

Published by Fawcett World Library, 67 West 44th Street, New York, N. Y. 10036 Printed in the United States of America

ARE YOU GOING TO NURSERY SCHOOL THESE DAYS, LUCY?

YES, I'VE BEEN REINSTATED

IS IT FUN?

IS IT FUN?! ALL WE HAVE TO DO EVERY DAY IS PLAY PLAY PLAY PLAY PLAY PLAY...

I'VE NEVER BEEN SO BORED IN ALL MY LIFE!

SCHULZ

WAIT A MINUTE! WHAT'S THIS?!

SNIF * SNIF*

ALL RIGHT! WHO PUT THE MOTH BALL IN THE RING?!

SCHULZ

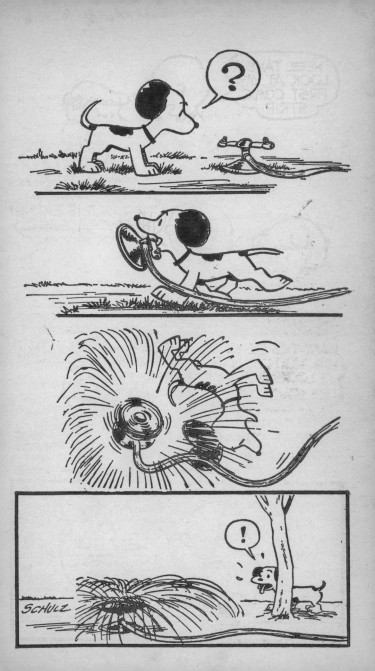